Robert Fulton
The Steamboat Man

Carin T. Ford

Enslow Publishers, Inc.

40 Industrial Road   PO Box 38
Box 398   Aldershot
Berkeley Heights, NJ 07922   Hants GU12 6BP
USA   UK

http://www.enslow.com

Library of Congress Cataloging-in-Publication Data

Ford, Carin T.
  Robert Fulton : the steamboat man / Carin T. Ford.
    p. cm. — (Famous inventors)
  Includes index.
  Summary: A brief biography of Robert Fulton, the inventor, artist, and engineer who is best known for his work with submarines and the steamboat.
  ISBN 0-7660-2248-X (hardcover)
  1. Fulton, Robert, 1765–1815—Juvenile literature. 2. Marine engineers—United States—Biography—Juvenile literature. 3. Inventors—United States—Biography—Juvenile literature. 4. Steamboats—United states—History—19th century—Juvenile literature. [1. Fulton, Robert, 1765–1815. 2. Inventors. 3. Steamboats—History.] I. Title. II. Series.
  VM140.F9F67 2004
  623.8'24'092—dc21   2003010141

Printed in the United States of America

10 9 8 7 6 5 4 3 2 1

To Our Readers: We have done our best to make sure all Internet Addresses in this book were active and appropriate when we went to press. However, the author and the publisher have no control over and assume no liability for the material available on those Internet sites or on other Web sites they may link to. Any comments or suggestions can be sent by e-mail to comments@enslow.com or to the address on the back cover.

Every effort has been made to locate all copyright holders of material used in this book. If any errors or omissions have occurred, corrections will be made in future editions of this book.

Illustration Credits: © 1999 Artville, LLC, p. 22; Architect of the Capitol, p. 28; Carnegie Library of Pittsburgh, p. 4; Collection of the New-York Historical Society, accession number 1967.48, negative number 47765, p. 19; Collection of the New-York Historical Society, negative number 50861, p. 16; Collection of the New-York Historical Society, negative number 71040, accession number 1924.7, p. 27; Collection of the New-York Historical Society, p. 1, 2, 13, 21; Enslow Publishers, Inc., p. 20; Independence National Historical Park Collection. Carrington Bowles, 1778 version of "An East Prospective View of the City of Philadelphia, in the Province of Pennsylvania, in North America, taken from the Jersey Shore" under the direction of Nicholas Scull, Surveyor General of the Province of Pennsylvania, p. 9; Lancaster County Historical Society, pp. 3, 6; Leila Cohoon, Leila's Hair Museum, p. 10; Library of Congress, pp. 15, 17; National Portrait Gallery, Smithsonian Institution/Art Resource, NY, p. 11; Oil painting by maritime historical artist William G. Muller, p. 25; Print Collection. Miriam and Ira D. Wallach Division of Art, Prints and Photographs. The New York Public Library. Astor, Lenox and Tilden Foundation, p. 23; Rebel Peddler, p. 26.

Cover Illustration: Lancaster County Historical Society (portrait). Spot art, from top right: Library of Congress, clipart.com, © 1999 Artville, LLC.

Table of Contents

Robert Fulton

Chapter 1

Young Inventor

obert Fulton had many ideas. From the time he was a young boy, he liked to invent things. One day, one of Robert's inventions saved him from getting into trouble. In those days, pencils cost a lot of money. So Robert figured out how to make one for himself.

On that day, he came to school late. The teacher was angry. Robert said he had been busy making lead for pencils. The lead is the black part that writes on the paper. Robert's teacher was so pleased with his pencil that he was not punished.

Robert was born in this house.

Many years later, Robert would become famous for his work with canals, submarines, and—most of all—steamboats.

Robert was born on November 14, 1765, on his family's farm near Lancaster, Pennsylvania. His parents were Robert and Mary Fulton. They had moved to the farm after living in the city of Lancaster for many years. Baby Robert had three older sisters: Elizabeth, Isabella, and Mary. Later, he would have a younger brother, Abraham.

Mr. Fulton had come to America from Ireland. At first, he worked as a tailor, sewing clothes for other people. Then he tried his luck as a farmer. But his crops did not grow well. After a few years, the family moved back to the city, and Mr. Fulton became a tailor again.

Lancaster was an exciting place for young Robert. There were so many different people—Scottish, German, French, African American. And the city was crowded with all sorts of interesting shops.

Robert started going to school when he was eight. In class, he did not always pay attention. Sometimes the teacher hit him across the hands with a cane.

When Robert was still a young boy, his father died. Robert's mother worked hard caring for her five children. The family did not have much money. Robert was eager to grow up and get a job. He wanted to earn money to help his family.

Chapter 2

Jewelry Maker and Artist

L ike many boys in those days, Robert's schooling ended when he was about fifteen years old. Then he became an apprentice to a jewelry maker in Philadelphia. An apprentice spent his days learning how to do a job from a skilled worker. He did not get paid. Instead, he was given food and clothing and a place to live.

Robert stayed there for several years. The jeweler

taught him how to make rings, necklaces, pins, and buttons out of silver. But Robert did not like this work. He was much happier drawing and painting.

After only two years, Robert left the jeweler's shop to become an artist. Robert painted very small pictures called miniatures. People bought them to hang on necklaces or wear on rings. It is thought that one famous person Robert painted was Benjamin Franklin.

Philadelphia was one of the biggest cities in America when Robert moved there.

This fancy wreath is made of human hair.

Robert also made tiny pictures out of human hair. This craft, called hairworking, was very popular. The hair could be twisted and woven into people, trees, ships, and other shapes. These, too, were worn on rings and necklaces.

When Robert was twenty-one, he became very sick. It is likely that he had a lung disease. He took a trip to West Virginia. Doctors hoped the fresh mountain air and water would help him get well.

When he was feeling better, Robert went back to Philadelphia. Then he sailed to London, England, to study art with Benjamin West, a famous painter. Soon, Robert began attending London's best art school, the Royal Academy of Arts. He earned some money by painting portraits of rich people. Over the years, some of his paintings were chosen for art shows at the Royal Academy. All his life, Robert would continue to paint pictures.

Robert knew he was a good artist, but not a great one. That was not enough for him. Most of all, Robert wanted to do something that would make him rich and famous.

Robert still liked learning about machines and how they work. In 1794, he won a medal for making a better machine to cut and polish marble. Robert decided to spend more of his time working with machines.

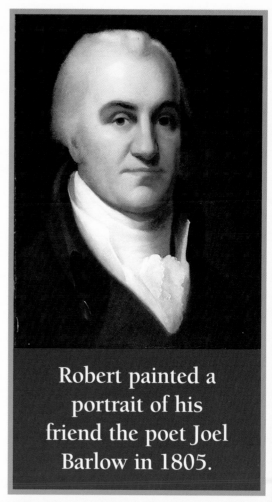

Robert painted a portrait of his friend the poet Joel Barlow in 1805.

Chapter 3

Working Abroad

Robert was interested in canal boats and canals. A canal is a man-made waterway that is dug out of the ground. Boats can travel along canals and rivers. In the days before trucks and highways, many businesses used boats to carry their goods to stores.

Robert traveled about England and studied a few canals. Then he drew up plans to make some changes in them. But no one cared about Robert's plans.

How could a boat travel up to a higher part of the canal? Robert had some ideas. He drew this picture of a boat being carried up a ramp.

When Robert was interested in something, he could not stop thinking about it. He kept working on ideas for better canals. He knew they were hard to dig. So he came up with an idea for a machine that could dig the soil and toss it to the side. It would be pulled by four horses.

Robert also wrote a book about how to make better canals. It was published in 1796, when Robert was thirty years old. Robert did not make any money from his book or his ideas. However, people now admired him for his skills as an engineer. An engineer is a person who designs and builds different kinds of structures and machines.

A Treatise on the Improvement of Canal Navigation by Robert Fulton, Jr.

Next, Robert traveled to France. He showed the French emperor his plans for a submarine, called the *Nautilus*. Submarines are boats that travel under the water. They had been

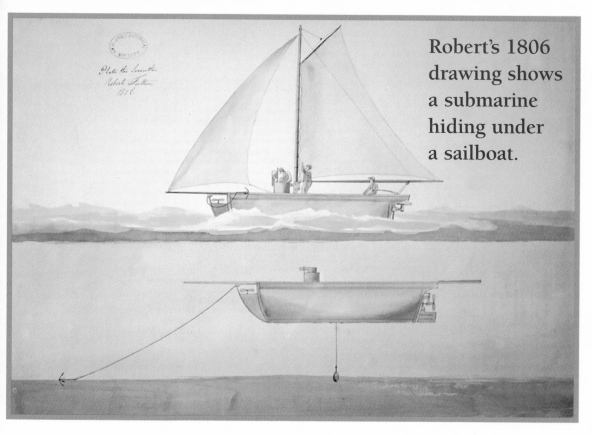

Robert's 1806 drawing shows a submarine hiding under a sailboat.

around since the 1600s. Robert's *Nautilus* was better because it could stay under water longer.

Robert also created a bomb that could be used underwater. At that time, France and England were at war. Robert told the French emperor that his submarine could carry these bombs and blow up English ships. But his plan failed, and the English war

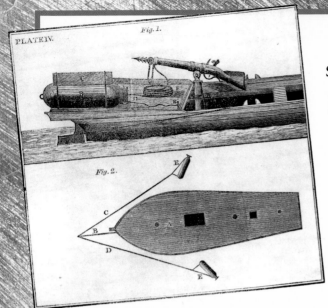

Here, Robert sketched more of his underwater bombs.

ships escaped without being hurt. The French lost interest in Robert's submarine.

Robert was working on other projects, too. He had heard about boats that could travel across the water using steam for their power. None of these boats worked very well. Robert's busy mind set to work. How could he make a better steamboat? By July 1803, Robert was ready to try out his steamboat on a river in France. It moved very slowly—just four miles an hour—but it worked.

The next year, Robert returned to England. The English government wanted Robert to use his submarine against French war ships. But once again, Robert failed to sink the enemy ships.

Robert was still interested in water travel. He kept working on plans for a better steamboat. In the fall of 1806, he sailed back to the United States. He knew just what he wanted to do. He would build a steamboat in America.

Robert drew a picture of himself looking out from a submarine.

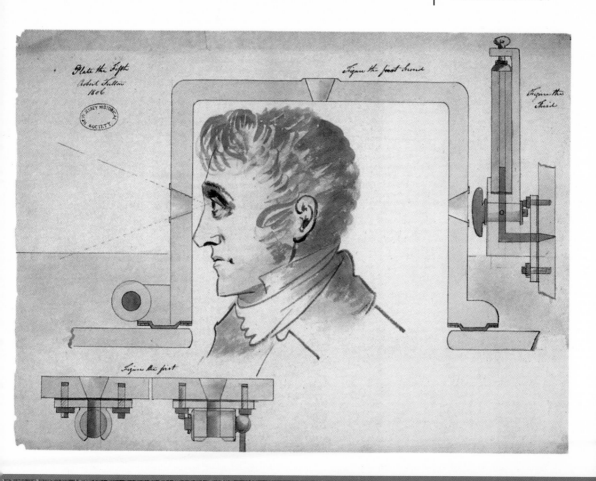

Chapter 4

"Fulton's Folly"

T he idea of a ship powered by steam had been around for hundreds of years. By the 1700s, many men were building steamboats. Yet most of these boats were not good for traveling. Their engines did not work well, and the boats moved very slowly. Worst of all, the steam engines often exploded.

There was a need for better transportation. Barges pulled by horses moved slowly. When farmers sent goods to market, the foods often spoiled along the way. Even the fastest sailing ships needed strong winds to move quickly through the water.

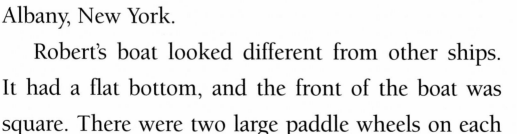

Robert made this portrait of himself for one of his friends.

Robert wanted to build a successful steamboat. His partner was Robert R. Livingston, an important man in the United States government. Robert Fulton had the ideas, and Robert R. Livingston had the money for their steamboat business. When their boat was ready, the two men decided to test it on the Hudson River. The steamboat would travel from New York City to Albany, New York.

Robert's boat looked different from other ships. It had a flat bottom, and the front of the boat was square. There were two large paddle wheels on each

Could a steam engine like this work well in a boat? Robert wanted to find out.

side of the boat. The steam engine made the paddle wheels turn. People did not believe it would work. They called it "Fulton's Folly" because they thought it was foolish.

On August 17, 1807, Robert's steamboat left New York City and began its 150-mile trip up the Hudson River. A crowd gathered to watch. No one believed a boat could go such a long distance powered by a steam engine. When black smoke poured out of the boat's chimney, most people were sure the steamboat would blow up.

The boat traveled almost five miles per hour. That was faster than most sailboats. There was a small crew on board. When the boat was halfway up the river, a farmer saw it. He was so frightened that he ran into his house and locked the doors and windows.

The steamboat arrived in Albany less than a day and a half later. It usually took ships four days to sail that far. An excited

Robert's first steamboat went up and down the Hudson River.

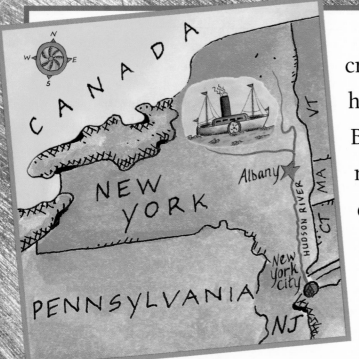

crowd was waiting at the harbor to greet the boat. But newspapers did not report the news. They did not think it was important.

Still, this did not bother Robert Fulton. He hung up a sign the very next day. For a small fee, anyone could travel back to New York City on his steamboat. Only two men were brave enough to go.

The next month, Robert's steamboat began to offer rides up and down the Hudson River. People were no longer afraid. The boat moved steadily through the water. Unlike sailing ships, the steamboat did not come to a stop when the wind stopped blowing. Robert's boat was a big success.

Robert named his boat the *North River Steam Boat*. North River was another name for part of the Hudson River. Later, Robert's steamboat was renamed the *Clermont*. Robert did not invent the steamboat, but he was the first to build a steamboat that worked well. He was also the first person to run a successful steamboat business.

Robert made traveling by steamboat fun and popular.

Success

Robert was earning money from the steamboat business. His boat carried people up and down the river. On one trip, there were 140 passengers on board.

Robert tried to make the *North River Steam Boat* as nice as possible. He had a cook, a waiter, and a large supply of food, such as chicken, beef, eggs, and watermelon. He wanted people to eat well and to have a good time.

The people on the *Robert Fulton* enjoyed
their trip on the Hudson River.

Robert also set up rules for the boat ride. Smoking was allowed only in certain areas, and women could not play card games after ten at night. No one could lie down with boots or shoes on. When passengers broke these rules, they had to pay a fine.

Robert's busy mind was always thinking of new ideas.

Whenever the steamboat needed repairs, Robert stayed calm. He never spoke harshly to his workers, and they admired him. One worker said that Robert was often deep in thought. He hardly noticed anything around him.

Robert had not lost interest in building and selling submarines and underwater bombs. This time, he hoped the United States government would want to buy them. He also thought more about canals. In

1808, he published a report on how canals would help the United States.

That same year, Robert married Harriet Livingston. She was twenty-four, and he was forty-two. When their first child was born, they named him Robert. The family lived in Washington, D.C., then moved to New York City. They had three more children, Julia, Mary, and Cornelia.

Robert fell in love with Harriet Livingston.

By 1811, Robert had built another steamboat in Pittsburgh, called the *New Orleans*. It traveled 2,000 miles down the Ohio and Mississippi Rivers. Over time, Robert would have many more steamboats traveling on American rivers. He also made a ferryboat to carry people between New York and New Jersey.

The next year, the United States fought against England in the War of 1812. Robert came up with a plan for a warship that was powered by steam. But he did not live to see this boat completed. When Robert was only forty-nine years old, he became very sick with pneumonia, a lung disease. He died on February 23, 1815.

One reason for Robert Fulton's great success was that he always made careful notes of his ideas. He built small models before making the full-size boats.

Robert Fulton was an artist, an inventor, and an engineer. He was a gentle man whose skill with machines helped change the way people traveled.

ROBERT FULTON

Timeline

1765~Born near Lancaster, Pennsylvania, on November 14.

1779~Begins work as an apprentice to a jeweler.

1787~Goes to England to study art.

1797~Travels to France and shows his plans for a submarine.

1802~Becomes partners with Robert R. Livingston to build a steam-powered boat.

1804~Returns to England and works on his underwater bombs.

1806~Sails back to America to build a steamboat.

1807~His first American steamboat leaves New York City on August 17 on the Hudson River.

1808~Marries Harriet Livingston on January 7.

1815~Dies on February 23.

Words to Know

apprentice—A worker who is learning a trade from a skilled worker.

canal—A waterway dug across land.

emperor—The ruler of an empire.

engineer—A person who knows how to design and build equipment, structures, and machines.

ferryboat—A boat to ferry (carry) people or things.

submarine—A boat that can travel under water.

War of 1812—A war fought between the United States and England from 1812 until 1815.

Learn More

Books

Quackenbush, Robert M. *Watt Got You Started, Mr. Fulton? A Story of James Watt and Robert Fulton*. Englewood Cliffs, N.J.: Prentice-Hall, 1982.

Schaefer, Lola M. *Robert Fulton*. Minnetonka, Minn.: Pebble Books, 2000.

Internet Addresses

The Legend of Steamboatin' the Rivers.
<http://www.steamboats.org/>

Steamboat Pictures and Information.
<http://www.johnhartford.com/steambt/steambt.htm>

Pennsylvania: Robert Fulton.
<http://www.robertfulton.org/>

Index